9x5

Patricia Callan
M.P. Carver
JD Debris
Catherine Fahey
Gregory Glenn

9x5

Copyright © 2022 by J.D. Scrimgeour, Editor

All rights reserved, including the right to reproduce this book or portions thereof in any form whatsoever without permission.

Contributors: Patricia Callan, M.P. Carver, JD Debris, Catherine Fahey, Gregory Glenn; All poems published with permission from the poets.

Cover image: "Family Wrangle at Picnic Place" by Quinton Oliver Jones, used with permission of his estate.

Book design: M.P. Carver, J.D. Scrimgeour, Brooke Delp
Layout: M.P. Carver
Copy Editing: Brooke Delp

Library of Congress Control Number: 2022903774
ISBN: 979-8-9858211-0-9
First Edition: 2022

Introduction by J.D. Scrimgeour 9

PATRICIA CALLAN

Mirrors 13
On My Eighteenth Birthday, My Friend Gave Me a Playgirl Magazine 14
Sappho in Dress with Pockets 16
Blue 17
Anesthesiologists Are the Sexiest Doctors 18
Boob Pantoum 20
Why I Bob My Daughter's Hair 21
There's an I.C.E. Center Behind the Burlington Mall 22
God Save 23

M.P. CARVER

C A P I T A L I S M 29
Black Thumbs 30
At the Public Housing Complex, or, It Wasn't All Bad Until We Ran Out of Sky 31
How to Enter the Trees 33
Epistle for William Lord (1931–2016) 34
Please bring: 35
The DJ asks 36
I try to resist the bird as soul metaphor 37
You Go, Girl 38

JD DEBRIS

The Voice of Hercules 43
Drunk With the Mermaid 47
On Future Rhyming Fuck You With Fuck You Four Times in a Row During "Rent Money" 48
Bossa Nova Was Invented in a Bathroom 51
Le Bonheur 52
New York, 2020 54
Beverly Grove 55
One for Adán 57
Those 'Mexicans For Golovkin' Shirts 59

CATHERINE FAHEY

Crewel 65
Gold as Straw 66
The Roses that Bloom at the End of the World 68
Inishmore 69
Ornithomancy 71
The External Soul 73
Queen of Swords 75
Page of Cups 76
Eight of Cups 77

GREGORY GLENN

wild 81
TV Dinner 83
Milhous 85
the Blender 87
Delta Sky Miles 90
Safe Outside 93
dog 94
Big Bird Singing at His Father's Funeral 96
Happy New Year from the Reptile Lagoon Dillon, SC 98

Acknowledgements 103
About the Poets 105

9x5

In the spring of 2017, I had a graduate poetry workshop that worked. The five poets in this collection were all in it, and we would often go out afterward to continue the conversation. I sense that they inspired each other. I know they inspired me.

Being an artist, wrote a young T.S. Eliot in "Tradition and the Individual Talent," involves a "continual extinction of personality." When I used to share Eliot's essay with my undergrads, they resisted this concept of depersonalization, which only made me believe in it more. Great art rises above the merely personal, right? Artists must learn how to distill their lives, their joys and pains, into something that isn't them. They must make themselves like that piece of platinum in Eliot's analogy. Unchanging itself, it enables elements to interact and make something new.

Well, whatever. That's a young man's game. When I read poetry now, I read for the voice, for companionship, for someone who wants to talk to me. What I appreciate about these poets is how their poems feel distinctly their own, how you couldn't mistake one for the other.

There's the wry wonder in the revels of M.P. Carver,
the thrill of someone tasting poetry's possibilities with Patti Callan,
JD Debris' personal mythologies, his hip elegies for masculinity,
the sting of Cathy Fahey's barbed lines,
and the hilarious melancholy of Greg Glenn.

It gives me joy to carry these poems with me, all in one lovely package, a present from the world.

J.D. Scrimgeour, 2022

PATRICIA CALLAN

Mirrors

My mother told me about a girl
who lost her arm in a fun house—

chopped off by a poorly
placed fan. She just walked

around bleeding, hypnotized
by her ruptured reflection;

sliced already into broken
girlhood, the loss of an

arm was imperceptible
amidst so much fracture.

On My Eighteenth Birthday, My Friend Gave Me a Playgirl Magazine

and a scratch ticket—
a kind but insensible gift since it was the
first day that I could have bought them for
myself. No stranger to the human
penis, I found it shocking, nonetheless—
over-exposed in glossy color.

Yet it elicited no other response, attached to a
man who was giving a bath (and other things)
to a woman who was not me, my ordinary narcissism
requiring both eye contact and at least the
vague possibility of mutual attraction.

The scratch ticket was a dud, too.

I love the internet, though—the rapidity
of change and the shiny new opinions.
I wonder if eighteen-year-olds still get porn
on their birthdays or if they ever get shocked
or bored, if they know how to doodle, or spell.

I think I'm forgetting.

I'm forgetting the first time I sounded out
the word "beaver" it was spread across
a woman's legs, wide in an open
magazine in my uncle's truck, how I

suddenly understood why my mother wanted me
to sit like a lady when I wore a dress.

.

Sappho in Dress with Pockets

You have drawn this line linking death and release—
thick and dark. So sharp is the drop in alti-
tude, so stark the shift from before to after,
no one could stop it.

In between, you fold and you stack. You pile neat
towers of wanting—pack up your organic
matter, pass whatever you have made off to
someone else, kind of

like the way you hand luggage to a bellhop.
Here, let all of us carry this for you. You
know how much we hold when we have to. Our whole
bodies are hands. But

could you leave us a finger or two to ourselves?
Could you just clear a space between the boxes of tapes
you mislabeled on purpose? We girls can create
as well as hold, we

conjure our release out of thin
air. We just need some air to do it.

Blue

I like the blueberries that are still purple,
which is not to say that I'm attracted to youth or the undeveloped.
I just like my fruit a little tart. On my honeymoon,
I ate passion fruit
and wondered if the Big Island water was too
vast for me, too blue.

Earlier that year, barefoot,
I looked up at your sigh from my barstool,
What do you want me to do? All you have to do is say it,
you said. But, of course, I wouldn't. Say it,

I mean. Not to you. I have never regretted silence. Isn't
that strange? The truths that I've spoken burst inside
out, like a jewel-weed's curls springing
off the tip of my finger.
I like to pull off the whole branch so
the delicate pod dangles, intact. I value the fragile
too highly, and the rare—every true thing can only
ever be revealed once.

Anesthesiologists Are the Sexiest Doctors

They cruise in while the others engage in injurious behavior
(Hippo-what-ic oath?) and make you feel good. That is their
whole job. They're like medical prostitutes, or overeducated
bartenders. And they're smooth bastards. They have far more
hair than men their age should be allowed, and they'll call you
"Sweetie" and you will definitely like it.

At first it's the world's saddest threesome, a pretty, but bored,
nurse holds your sweating face in her soft hands—foreheads
touching—while he's back there finding his favorite vertebra.
You're not wearing any underwear but you are wearing hair-pins which
will be the subject of great debate—are these allowed? The nurse
is unsure but this guy has never been unsure about anything.
He thinks your hair looks great—don't change a thing.

He's a talker, and his voice is the only sound that ever mattered. Joni
Mitchell's "A Case of You?" Just a mosquito buzzing in your ear. Your
daughter's laugh? Like the sound of your car refusing to turn over at 6am.
This first medication might make you a little nauseous so please let him know…
Oh it does, it does, please fix it (your release from each new torture
depends upon this magnificent stranger) *please fix it.*
He fixes it, penetrates your spinal fluid with more skill than force.

The surgeons come in, and he stands by you since your husband is not
allowed in yet. Husband? What husband? I mean, you remember a
honeymoon and some nights when he made you feel pretty damn good,
but not direct-to-the-brainstem-good. Not paralyzed-from-the-shoulders-
down-good. Not good enough to sustain the excitement of being
sliced open while wide awake.

Your best friend is this Earth Mother Fertility Goddess who pushed her drug-free babies into the world on a yoga ball from her magical elastic vagina. But you had little to do with your baby's birth, extracted and rescued by a stranger, then passed to five sets of other people's hands.

That anesthesiologist was all yours, though, the last to put your needs first, to induce rest in a restless moment,
your handsome defender against the tiny assassin in your womb.

Boob Pantoum

She drank
and my daughter bounced as I laughed

at her wide-mouthed grin on my nipple. Even
good and smart men still sometimes lose focus

if my breasts bounce as I jump,
which isn't often, but I'm afraid I'm a

good and smart woman who still sometimes
forgets that jumping is a performance.

It isn't often that I'm afraid, but once
I fed my daughter in a Panera,

forgetting that skin is a performance, too.
A man stood behind and looked over my shoulder and

stared at my daughter in that Panera,
and at my wide-eyed fear of his eager grin. Yet even

as the man stood behind and looked over my shoulder,
she drank.

Why I Bob My Daughter's Hair

I skimmed, with a comb, her rippling
highest point, but she wasn't ready.

Knots be damned, I slit the
center of each cord until it was

two,
three,
twelve,
eighty-thousand

separate threads baring
only teeth between them.

One day her screams will require
something sharper, a horizontal attack.

A trunk full of what used to be
her, what used to be her lace curtain,

will sit patiently in the corner of all those
moments she hates me the most.

There's an I.C.E. Center Behind the Burlington Mall

you don't have a backyard so your aunt
drives forty minutes to the beach at Lynch Park
at seven in the morning on the fourth of July
to save a place for half your family to set up
the barbecue while the other half is still in
Guatemala and you start digging giant holes in the sand
to fill with tiny oceans before the fireworks start
so all your cousins can sit in the water and watch
and when a little white girl starts building a castle
next to you you invite her to help even though
she is so quiet and a little strange and isn't your cousin
and lives here near the water all year and you say
she's lucky even though she has no cousins at all

God Save

Amelia has a life-sized
wax sculpture of the Queen
of England in her living room.
She was shipped from a museum
in Amsterdam where Dutch lips
kissed off the paint around
her Majesty's mouth, leaving her
looking like the day after Halloween.

Her royal highness wears a
hand-me-down suit and pearls
but no crown. She holds a cup
of tea as she sits, surrounded
by chew toys and furniture built
by Amelia's husband forty
years ago, when he could still see.

We aren't the kind of gilded,
eccentric street on which
one might expect to find such
an artifact displayed.
We're all little, and tidy,
everyone with the same
pumpkins on their front steps.

Someday, I'll have to find
Elizabeth a home. She has
no children, no living relatives
at all. Just a little dog, the

oldest house on our street, and
the smooth, ageless finish of
a woman who will never die.

M.P. CARVER

CAPITALISM

My nephew's not even three yet
but already he can spell some words
like S A L E and M A L L
and I'm glad he's picking up
the finer nuances of capitalism
along with his letters.

If I can't give him a better world
at least he can play with this one.
It's like when you buy toddlers
the best Christmas presents
and they spend the whole day
playing pretend with the box.

It's an ailing metaphor
but modern culture's like the box.
I think of Ke$ha as a box.
I really like Ke$ha.
She's probably for sale
not that it does me any good.

If I could buy Ke$ha
I don't think we'd be happy
but we could both make-believe for a while.
We wouldn't even have to kiss
but after we could sit side by side
and watch even the sun depreciate.

Black Thumbs

This is a poem about finding
contentment in the garden, about
my life both budding and rotting away
and all the mundane language
carrying me from point A →
to nothing-particularly-striking sunset B.
But this isn't just about me!

You too can bury the things you dreamed
about in the dirt, where they churn
into sprout, edible, stir-fry, and then shit.

Did evolution create this? The chance
and change of heritable characteristics
tangling up unto eternity? Or some God?
Half-hearted creator of your drooping
azaleas, the whole sad world of beauty?

My friends, here's the truth:
even He didn't think
you were meant
for the garden.

At the Public Housing Complex, or, It Wasn't All Bad Until We Ran Out of Sky

That summer we made
our parents go check
the basement because
we swore we'd seen
a homeless guy sneaking
in and out. They didn't
find him or believe
us, but later a smelly bucket
proved we weren't lying.
I remember the landlord
would come rolling in
for a visit in a shiny car
each Sunday and park it
in our rusting sea
of jalopies. He didn't kick
anyone out for paying
late and got broken
appliances fixed right
away by his son-and-law
who came quick to hit
on all our single moms.
We were afraid to touch
the baby birds we found
chirruping in the back yard
bushes, and at night
bats coming out to eat
the mosquitoes would swoop

right down in front
of our faces. We learned
to trick them
into going after any
small enough thing
thrown up into the air.
I wonder what those
poor bats thought
of it all? The toil, the
expectations, the pebbles?

How to Enter the Trees

In the space   between
 one oak and the next, in the
  birches, the coyotes are waiting.
   Coyotes: terrible.   Full of teeth
    & intent, end quotes & maelstroms.   This is
     what it means to be in the woods, to
      be soft, poetic, full of speech & filaments.   What
       is nature?   The space my heart carves
        on the page as my skin crawls through the air.   The
         birth of even so much as dread & the Romantics.   Poets
          all around, bark & abrasion, human eyes entering
           the space between the conifers, the maples, the pines.   Talk
            from the open cavern of the sky.   Swallow & pretend
             to know the names of things, to walk upright, to sing songs.   About
              us, the firs drop sharp tin needles in the flimsy, unlasting light.

Epistle for William Lord (1931–2016)

I don't know what to say to you. How
have you liked the weather up there?
I poured my guts out into those clouds
and into explaining the thermostat each
and every morning for three years.
Your memory was pretty ragged,
but it could have been worse. I was glad
for the stroke, though it was terrible.
Up there, can you tell what is the sky
from what is the emptiness inside the sky?
Are you still having trouble with the t.v.?
Press the big red button on the right.
I'm sorry for the last crappy nursing home
when all the money was gone. What exactly
is my tone here? And is it to you
that I'm writing? I was always a talker,
a babbler really, you'd tell me to *slow down
speak clearly*. Sometimes I think the voice
in my poems is that one you helped me
step outside of. Should I thank you? In the end,
you babbled too, and I had no voice to give you.
I miss you. I remember, that's what I wanted
to say, and my voice gets stronger every day.
Carry on, don't come down on my account,
you're doing great. Or at least you're doing
exactly as well as they said you would.

Please bring:

- A single red rose, to break the ice
- €2000, cash or credit accepted
- Detailed medical history
- 3x5 headshots of each of your exes, excluding those already dead, ordered from most to least attractive
- 1 piece sea glass, blue preferred
- **At least** three open dreams, signed & notarized
- 1 lead butterfly
- Teeth as preferred, not to exceed 33
- Glow in the dark plastic stars
- Number two pencil, sharpened
- The memory of the smell of gasoline
- Candied pomegranate
- Lust
- 1 set synthetic bones
- Yellow leaves, pressed dry in the pages of a textbook
- Names and phone numbers of those you have damaged irreparably, if any
- Desperation
- Iced coffee, black
- 108 grains of green sand from a board game hourglass
- 1 subconscious, fully emptied
- Itemized fears
- Claw marks gouged in **either** flesh **or** stone
- Your mother's scar
- A full accounting of unpaid debts, to be weighed
- Your best salt & pepper shakers
- A street sign stolen from your hometown
- 13 poems with questionably effective metaphor, like black bristles through so much red paint

...en he repeats

...y'all doing tonight? And so I reply:

I have felt a darkness
putting up roots
through the arches
of my feet, and moving
along the worn paths
of my own veins
and capillaries, and now,
each year, this heaviness
blots out more
of what I once
did not know
to call light.

The DJ has no more questions.

I try to resist the bird
as soul metaphor

but watching them there, soaring,
scuffling over trash,
chasing each other off
lampposts in the grey
dawn of the all-night
Dunkin' Donuts parking lot—
I'm moved
despite myself.

You Go, Girl

If I lined up all my money in singles the long way
I'd have almost 1/10th of a mile of cash.

Enough to take me from my door
to the candy aisle of the Walgreens.

The short way, I can make it to the parking garage,
but I can't pay the meter.

I have 988 grams of money,
or I would, if money weren't theoretical.

Instead I have pixels that The Bank is loaning to me
in exchange for my money, Dear Green Hostage.

Either they don't want to negotiate
or my ransom note got lost in the mail.

They cut the letters from *Fortune* magazine,
arranged them with an eye for aesthetics,

then charged the cost of the materials, labor, and a stamp
to my account—I think the teller did it.

But I don't blame her; it was a creative project.
It was art. She loved it.

And even factoring in the fees,
I can still get to the sliding glass doors of the Walgreens.

JD DEBRIS

The Voice of Hercules

Remembering that heavyweight
we'd call Hercules,
a mellow steroid fiend
who never sparred, just raised

barbells 'til he was swollen as that solemn
British killer from *Ninja 2: Shadow
of a Tear*. He'd flex, hit vacuum
poses in ringside mirrors, taking photo

after photo, & lounge in the locker room,
nothing but a sideways Sox hat on.
A garden-variety goon
with a garbled, guttural monotone

& shriveled steroid balls:
so Hercules seemed, on the surface.
But every word he spoke was praise—
"So sick, bro"—softly, near-inaudible.

One night, the gym screened a pay-
per-view—De la Hoya or Money May.
All us gym rats came back
in jewelry, jeans, & the reek

of cologne instead of sweat
to cozy up between dormant
heavy bags & watch the fights
projected on industrial concrete.

I brought my old acoustic
for between-fight amusement,
background-strumming a soundtrack
to our cacophony. Hercules sat

beside me, saying, "Bro,
can you play a corrido beat?"
I started to strum a stock waltz-meter,
& Hercules, in a bass bel canto

that could rumble the cheap seats
of an opera hall, began a Spanish ballad
about a lost bantamweight
named Amen, who had disappeared,

the lyrics went, to Mexico last spring,
whom no one had heard from since.
The gym was quiet one verse in.
Pay-per-view muted, everyone listening

to this supposed bonehead
channel beauty. To his ballad,
its fragility—Fly,
little dove, fly, he'd sigh

at verses' end. I'm amazed
that no one laughed at him—
insults, back then, our lingua
franca & form of praise—

in that moment so holy
& ridiculous, when his lips formed O's
on long, pure
tones, & every chord

perfectly—somehow—
harmonized.
I can't tell you which prize-
fighter won that bout,

or if we gorged on pizza & beer,
blowing off our weight-making regimens.
I can't tell you if it rained, I can't pretend
to know if sparks flew inside all those ears

bent in unison toward the amen
Hercules incanted. As for him,
his trainer, a hardass marine,
got sick of his preening

& told him go find another gym
where he could kiss his biceps
in the mirror, & drink his creatine
& beast his endless deadlift reps.

How many songs has he sung since,
in the shower of a distant gym
where he still takes his sweet time
soaping every ropelike vein?

What I know, I'll tell:
around the campfire of the muted fights
that night, he was our horn of Gabriel,
our nightingale mid-flight.

Sing it again, Hercules?
                    "Aight."

Drunk With the Mermaid

"The bottom of the sea is less cruel than you'd think,"
she tells me, four drinks deep at *The Schooner Hannah*
(the dive bar, not the boat), leaning in to play with the links

of my secondhand crucifix. She's the great-great-grand-
daughter of shipwrecked Cape Verdean whalers
who didn't drown, somehow, but instead built, from wet sand,

tidewrack, driftwood & clamshell, houses at the sea's nadir.
They fell for subaquatic fiancées & interbred, she tells me,
making a life in which they were the Ishmaels, the narrators,

not the interchangeable extras x-ed out of early
Melville revisions. She sounds like distant windchimes
when she exhales, & what I thought were a few stray

curls are really cursive, f-shaped slits below her jawline.
Weirdly familial five drinks deep, I think of my sister,
who, though not half-amphibian, fish, or dolphin,

is half-Polish & can swim like a motherfucker.
Me, I just sink.
                    She parts the dive bar's beaded curtains,
leads me down cobblestone streets to the pier,

& swan-dives in the harvest moon's reflection, extending
stone-smooth, polished fingers through the glint.
The bottom of the sea is less cruel than you'd think.

Future Rhyming Fuck You With Fuck You Four Times in a Row During "Rent Money"

I want you to hear this and be like, "Man, he gave us all of him. He let everything out."
—Future

There's more church in a one-note drone on my collaborator's organ-
simulation software than I've seen the inside of this year. Origin

stories bore me to tears, but let's say *fuck it* & start back in the barrio:
Summers I'd shoot hoops in a fútbol-only barrio,

have languid lonely shootarounds at caged-in Constitution Beach,
rapping along to my boombox, going silent on every *motherfucker* or *bitch*

for fear of retribution. God was still listening then. I stayed close to sunstroke,
shooting endless threes, my release point smoothed to butter. Never had a sweeter stroke

& no one around to see it. Well, there *was* the occasional five-on-five
among full-grown men, but my jump shots all got swatted. Wasn't even five

feet tall then, weighed less than a sweat-soaked towel thrown over a park bench.
What I loved, way more than full-court—with its trash talk, thrown elbows, constant bench-

riding, & Beckett-lengths of waiting to sub in—& even more than solitude, were shootarounds
in tandem, trio, quartet. Once a young Matheus came around,

a Matheus I'd never met, would never see again. Brazilian, lanky, braids
hanging past his neck, I remember watching him leap to grab the long, white, braided

x-stitch of the net (it glowed pristine, as if City Parks, at dawn, had changed it); I remember him pulling & pulling until it ripped from the rim

& how he seemed to do it for no reason.
Everything, then, happened for a reason.

The rhythm of dribble/brick/pavement/rim paced
the conversation—between the ball's bright *pings* or over a no-look pass

we'd say our piece. Matheus dished a rumor about a Boston
Latin soccer star, why he retired aged sixteen: "Bro, he busted

inside his girl without a condiment. Now he's got a *sex disease*."
Just as likely: the dizzy

spells of a surprise first trimester, the high school winger quitting, picking up full-time
shifts at a Revere Beach roast beef stand. Or maybe just running. Time

is money, Heidegger, I believe, wrote. Your baby mama fucks me better when the rent's due,
Future rapped, & do I believe them dudes?

Truth be told, I slipped a hundred & two fifties into a single mother's handbag at age twenty-one, told her "Baby, get your braids done." She just handed

back the cash, closed my fist, & patting it whispered, "Keep it, boy. Your rent's due."
The fantasy & its own undoing:

that silver might drip from a neck bitten or a back clawed hard enough. For just one faux-sure
sentence, let me envision what happened to varsity winger & wifey, fucking away one future

as they improvised another; let me envision the fruit of their improvisation full-
grown now, throwing elbows in a full-

court game of beachfront five-on-five, banging on the worn-paint asphalt. The same court
where I once shot jumpers with switchblade-thin Marselly & her older cousin Courtney,

both shrink-wrapped in Brazilian jeans, their gold hoop earrings untouchable & distant
as the rim. A drizzling Monday, seagulls in the distance,

the matching cousins' snapping gum, their *mierda*s every time they missed.
They asked me why I didn't swear, & in what today I might consider a misstep, some mystic

shit, or simply a "missed shot," I told them I'd made a contract with God.
Nowadays, I can't get through a prayer without a few *fucks* for emphasis, just ask God.

Nowadays, I'm convinced any word that keeps repeating
& repeating is a prayer. Like when Future finds an end-line *fuck you* & repeats it

till it's mantra.
    So, broken courtside boombox, go on whispering through your landfill *yes yes*
  y'all & you don't stop.
& Future, autotuned, on cough syrup, on loop, rhyming *fuck you* with *fuck you* till eternity: don't
  stop.

Bossa Nova Was Invented in a Bathroom

The samba would no longer shower

                                        (João Gilberto spoke only in whispers)

He hid behind the drawn curtains of the samba

                                        (Two chords droning the samba's silk unraveled)

He holed up in his sister's flat in Diamantina

                                        (He paid his rent in tangerines)

He was, like the green-eyed monastery wolves, nocturnal

                                        (All to echo the washerwomen's rhythm at the river)

The piled-up laundry was a sculpture of Medusa

                                        (Remembering washboards, silks, & wicker)

His *bim bom*s ping-ponged off brittle, porcelain hexagons

                                        (Drain flies buzzed across nasal harmonics)

The balladeer must go DOWN to THE RIVER ad infinitum

                                        (A faucet is no less a river than a river)

Le Bonheur

(*for Agnès*)

The weekend Agnès Varda died, you matched me
drink for drink in my attic-kitchen—one overflowing
skull-chalice of RELAX rosé for every whiskey-
ginger I ingested. In 1965, Agnès Varda shot a film
called *Happiness*, & like so many other early mornings,
that is what we drank & laughed to—near-delirium.

Told the story of trekking once from Central,
stopping for after-work cigars at Leavitt & Peirce,
then on to Harvard to hear Agnès Varda lecture.
Exhaling toxins by the Church St. exit, an Escalade
pulls up. A sunglassed, slicked, & suited chauffeur
extends a hand to abuelita Agnès, who eases

down, step by careful step, from SUV to ground.
There goes the godmother of the *Nouvelle Vague*,
winking at us as she passes! The story might as well end
right there (before I start fawning), with *the gesture*,
which is cinema, which is your arms around my neck
as you kiss me on a kitchen chair. I don't remember

if I said this two or three drinks later,
but here's what I got from *Le Bonheur*.
It's all sunflowers & Mozart until somebody breaks
a vow. For now, we're all overtime shifts, irregular gigs,
kisses between cracks in the hustle. My cinema?
It's the sunrise & half-shut eyes through which

I watch you stretch, smooth shea butter over right
leg, then left. A goodbye kiss & you're off to catch
the bus in sky-blue scrubs. Another shooting script:
you, scarved in silk against the pillowcase, streetlights
liquid through the blinds, I brush your forehead,
go chase a check across the bridge. Coming back

to find you in my sweats in front of mango peels
& an open endocrinology text, Bobby "Blue" Bland
from your facedown phone, your soft & citrus breath, your nasal
off-key hum-along, your thumb on a diagram of the adrenal gland.
Agnès was right, irising out to brightness between each scene—
before black, we fade to every color we can name.

New York, 2020

from "Chalino Sánchez: A Sequence"

Chalino Sánchez Félix, you should be living this hour
when our borderline's barbed wire crawls vining
across a throat, when its shadows fall in spirals, & tighten.

The corrido begins like this: declare you're
about to sing one—*voy a cantar*. First verse,
Glock against the smuggler's jaw. Ford Conquistador

speeding away in the second. Third & final, as silver
trumpets sway, you hear tall pines crying on their ridge.
But before all that, the corrido begins in commerce:

barter a crime lord's tribute song for a pistol or a crucifix,
lionize a henchman for a ram's horn stuffed with twenties.
& long before all those beginnings, this:

you kill your sister's rapist at an all-night party.
You cross a border. You're fifteen, invincible & cursed.

Beverly Grove

from "Chalino Sánchez: A Sequence"

I wanted café con leche, a little peace,
when I stopped into that coffeeshop on Third
with nothing but a notepad in my western shirt
& a corrido I half-finished months back in La Mesa.

What was I doing in that gabacho neighborhood?
Well, that's for me to know & the law to guess!
Fine, I was just at Bloomingdale's, nothing badass—
bought the wife a ruby crucifix bright as blood.

Blonde barista rapid-fired some English,
mirrored my smile. I asked for (I thought) coffee,
got some iced swill sweet as Fanta, weak as tea.
Took a corner seat & started scribbling

notes on Armando's murder—seven bullets,
messenger dove singing bad news over Sanalona,
his sons (my nephews) all fatherless & grown—
when the boss stormed out from ensconcement

to knock knuckles on my tabletop, red-jowled.
Maybe he didn't like me leaning back in snakeskin,
cowboy boots crossed on a chair, shirt unbuttoned,
or the tilt of my Tejana brim, how its shadow fell.

In that half-finished corrido, Armando, lionhearted
even through his execution at the Santa Rita hotel,
would've flipped the table, made this gringo piss himself.
Me? Parolee from La Mesa, trying not to be deported,

I bit my tongue until the song beneath it bled.
I wrapped my song in fabric el jefe could never pull off,
in a language he'd never comprehend, & left.
Raising a middle finger instead of my dead.

One for Adán

from "Chalino Sánchez: A Sequence"

What ridiculous luck to even be born.
What ridiculous luck, living long enough to sing
how your father was murdered by false policemen.
What ridiculous luck to make it through the chorus,

the next measure, next note, through the breath
before the downbeat, the 'yes' that one lung says
to its twin. Adán, what, if anything, brings us together?
Arbitrary borders, a belief in curses, folk saints

who steal from the rich. Aunts, sisters, & mothers
who've suffered too damn much. A brass band
is passing. I'm back on my grandfather's shoulders
in Fall River, Mass. It's Festa do Espirito Santo,

& a sousaphone gives heartbeats to the Virgin
Mary float, cymbals clashing… Yes, Chalino met
his badge-flashing, sunglassed assassins outside Culiacán,
yes, your limo crashed in that same free & sovereign state,

& no, I can't match the pitch of fifteen thousand
teenagers weeping in the streets of Los Angeles,
or the mess that followed—riot gear & pellet guns,
Ford truck flipped over, in flames. But ridiculous

luck, Adán, is needed for one's own voice to adorn,
postmortem, a few romantic ballads in a locked room—
Nadie es Eterno, Bésame Morenita—where two, in candlelight,
can create anything: even a little death, even a life.

Those 'Mexicans For Golovkin' Shirts

from "Chalino Sánchez: A Sequence"

A bootleg of a bootleg of a bootleg.
Red screen print on polycotton blends

fallen off the back of a truck.
Juan & I hawked seven boxes

outside Madison Square Garden
the night Gennadiy Golovkin

knocked out David Lemieux.
Some photos could outlive Lascaux's

charcoal, oxide, & ocher: Chalino
at the table with the cocked Tejana,

shirt unbuttoned, loading the Glock.
Some rando photoshopped the Kazakh

killer Golovkin's goofy grin onto
our narco-icon. We caught on pronto,

printed up a ream, sold Sánchez's silhouette
the same way he once sold cassettes,

on the street. Then counted twenties
on the almost-empty Queensbound E,

where, every morning, an accordion
player wanders car to car & keens.

CATHERINE FAHEY

Crewel

As I thread the needle in my eye,

you pout, *I don't understand.*

Nevertheless, I invite you
closer to see the scars
stitched on my freckled canvas.

There is beauty
in the making, I say.

You say I should stay sunny,
so I embroider the moon on my hand.

Gold as Straw

It starts with sheep. Prosaic,
unmagical sheep. Shearing,
washing fleeces. Picking
out shit and grease and plants, saving
whatever wool is left. Spend
winter carding, combing. Thinking
there is nothing else.

Walking back and forth
at the great wheel, spinning
fluff into form, wearing
a trough in the ground. Knowing
exactly how saints are broken by wheels.

Spinning done between
other chores: cooking, washing, feeding, tending.
Gendered work, it's easy
to scratch your hand
on the great iron spindle, get sepsis, die.

Spinning, dyeing, weaving, knitting, fulling, sewing, fitting, mending rags.
Hands are a channel for thread.
My shuttle doesn't fly, just falls.
My needle won't guide a prince to my door.

It's never enough for my father.
It's never enough for my husband.
It's never enough for *him*.

You, listening to my stories,
Do you even ask my name?

The Roses that Bloom at the End of the World

are $5.99 at Trader Joe's.
They come wrapped in cellophane, surrounded
by leatherleaf ferns, with a futile packet of plant food.

I place the roses in a milk glass vase on the windowsill
behind the sofa, so the cat can enjoy them, too.
It's not her fault the world is ending.

The roses that bloom at the end of the world
are hybrid—all vibrant colors,
no scent, no thorns. I'm not worried
about the cat swallowing a thorn,
or the vet bill.

I place the vase on the windowsill,
framed by the curtains, so the neighbors
can see them, too. They should enjoy this
last chance for gossip while
they can. Busybodies to the end.

The roses that bloom at the end of the world
last long enough. It's their job—to stay
with us. To watch, to wait
to witness. To say
yes there was a world
and yes there was a life
and yes that is over now and

Inishmore

A 5,000-year-old ring fort defends the cliff
from invaders, its stones

offering little protection to tourists.
So you crawl along the drop.

There's nothing for you at home. Your parents
sold the house your freshman year;

you came back at Thanksgiving break
to a cot in a basement.

Now, standing on the western edge of Europe—
no one would notice if you were pushed, or if you fell.

You came here to find yourself—
you tried on different names: one week Catherine,

another Kate. You changed behaviors
as you changed names.

You've sent out hundreds of résumés.
You're living here on the last dollars

of subsidized student loans.
The government owns your brain.

Below you, a solitary cranesbill, pink petals
blooming against the gray waves,

and bright it clings to the cliff face;
braver and more content than you.

You came to Ireland to find yourself—
to lose yourself.

You got drunk on Redbull and vodka,
spent the night with a boy

in a squeaky hostel bed, uncomfortable
in your skin and his hands.

Now it's you and the cranesbill,
dangling on the edge of potential.

It's 100 meters to the ocean below,
3,000 miles to Boston.

It's 7 kilometers to the ferry
and back to Galway.

Ornithomancy

After "Largo Dolcemente con Assarezza ma con Amaleleta" by Quinton Oliver Jones

A murmuration of starlings
in the shape of a bird
is an omen
        of an omen,
the Magic 8-Ball saying
"Ask again later,"
shuffling tarot cards, dealing
The Fool, The Fool, The Fool.

A murmuration in the shape
of anything else
can be interpreted.
        Inauguration
is to take omens from birds
in flight, ancient priestesses
seeking proof of worthiness
in public officials.
        What does it mean
when a congress of crows, all
self-important black feathers,
sits in judgement over a senate
of seagulls, fat and greasy, accused
of stealing from a committee
of vultures?
        What does it signify
when a starling shits
on a politician?

On Inauguration Day, all
the birds, waxwings, woodthrushes,
catbirds, barn swallows, great
herons and common grackles, arrange
themselves on bare branches and
power lines, settle in, tune
their chirping. They become
notes on staves,
        notating
their own sounds in common
harmony across habitats. Conducting
the forest, dictating
descant, counter-rhythm,
bass line. The aural arrangement
of self, of self embirded
as augury.

        Suddenly,
the flock takes flight,
resettles, writes a new song,
tells a different future.

The External Soul

I read a fairy tale, or think I did, about a giant
who kept his heart in an egg, and could not die.
Best practice is to have on-site and external
backups of all data, but I'm leery
of accidental custard, so I save my mind
in multiple redundancies.

My strongest memories are cast in metal.
The silver and green earrings are souvenirs of Ireland,
and the gold sun-and-moon ones hold
a dream. That bracelet was made on a dare.
When I wish to forget, I follow
KonMari, and thank
the object for its service.

I sold my high school ring for scrap
because I hated those bitches, and kept
my sorority pin, even though I de-sistered:
a charm against future bitches. My mother's
class ring sits in my jewelry box,
its onyx stone cracked, half-missing. I can't
bring myself to wear it, look at it, destroy it,
sell it, toss it into the sea, bury it, burn it.
So I hide it away, and keep it close.

I never got a college ring, for those years
are kept in books. Tangled together,
their plots and theses jumbled into
journals and mixtapes and souvenir t-shirts. I read

...logical study that says we misname
...people we love because our brains store
...important names in the same place. When I call
you Frodo, it's not because I'm losing
my mind, think you're a hobbit, or
love the dog more.

Everyday memories—ice cream & dances,
bike rides & red lights, my nieces' screams,
my sister's hair—are planted
in a field. They grow wild there,
among rosemary for remembrance &
pansies for thoughts & rue for
fuckups, all transformed, passing
from bee to bee, becoming
honey-sweet and candle-light.

The hardest memories, the ones
I can't stop thinking about, the ones
I can't tell my therapist, the ones
I can't trust in my head, or outside it,
are forget-me-nots, tattooed on my hands.

Queen of Swords

Write. Write through mattress-fog, cotton-headed
depression. Write through mania, you manifesting
Maenad-Medusa-Medea. Write with your misfiring
neurons, pull the sword from your brain and let
the grey matter drip words and letters on the page.

Write. Sounds breathe words breathe back
to your story, your beginning. Write until your
hands cramp and the pencil nubs. Write
again. Write with paper, with actions, with breath.

Write. Write with your fingers and tongue. Let
the words scab like blood. Find meaning in thorn-pricks,
cat scratches, cutting. Let the scars tell their stories.

Write. Create your real. You're
the sharp edge of the blade and the hilt in your hand.

Ace of Cups

I stand in the ocean in the rain.
The incoming tide laps my ankles
while the raindrops beat arhythmically
on my head. There is no moon,
only streetlights. Airplanes,
against velvet clouds, play the part
of stars. I reach down,
cup my hands, pour ocean water over
my head. Twice. A third time. Salt
and fresh water mix with my own tears.
I wash and renew myself to the chorus
of semi-truck and police siren,
of rain hitting pavement, puddles, ocean,
sand, leaves, rocks, flesh.

Eight of Cups

I don't know why I'm crying, whether it's
for me or us or the onions. The TV
plays a never-ending *Law & Order*
marathon, and the washing machine is
spinning, spinning. I wrap my expectations
in silk, tied with ivy, bandaged with yew.
That parcel sits on the table, next to
the thawing steak, the patient vegetables.
I'm chopping and crying, harder now—I've
cut my fingers, leaving a trail of blood
through the kitchen. All I need is my phone,
passport and purse. All that's left is to leave
the keys in the lock, ghost through the door, and
turn my face to the solace of the moon.

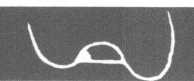

GREGORY GLENN

wild.

and then there was this person that didn't know
they were at the end of things. and they were making their way through
what now seemed like a desert.

oh sure, along the way there had been some bursts of life, some freckles
of action, and some dreams and some fireworks,
a little icing and a little gravy.

you can go crazy wondering if you're good or bad,
or if it's all been worth it to show up and to
make it through and to get on and get there.

wondering if it's really a desert, or a beach,
or if it's a playground,

and here there was an old metal slide with two buzzards on it,
and the buzzards looked at this person looking back at them.
none of these three had any desire in their eyes, or any
surprise.

now the person asked "what was I ever, to anyone?"
and the buzzard on the left, a stoic, leaned down:

"the truth is a thing that at birth may seem invisible to the eye,
and recognizable to the heart. toward the end the truth may
seem visible to the eye but unrecognizable to the heart. but it exists
always, and always inside of us, between the eyes and the heart,
and it is complex, winding and living inside you so deeply that
you yourself become complex, winding and hidden inside yourself.
and it is in this way that you are like a duck's penis."

then the person died.
and then the two buzzards looked at the dead person there.

the other buzzard, the one on the right, that one said,
"why do you always tell them that? why is it always this duck penis stuff with you?"
and the first buzzard said "i dunno just something to think about.
i mean have you ever seen a duck's penis before?
god damn. they're just wild."

TV Dinner

hey so there was a bunch of pigs standing around eating
a bunch of corn that was thrown out for them to eat,
and they happily ate it and you could tell they were
happy on account of their tails curlying and cueing,
and all the sounds that they made while they were
eating the corn and a few of the pigs were watching
two pigs fighting over a corn cob even though there was
plenty of other corn around for them to eat, and
the pigs watching them were enjoying the fight even
though it was kind of upsetting that the two pigs
would fight each other like this, and then a thought
occurred to one of the pigs watching and it said: "hey
everyone if I could just have your attention for a second,
I wonder what you all think, that if Christ had been
an animal, what kind of animal do you suppose he
would have been?" and the other pigs started to think
about it, except the two fighting pigs, and then as
the other pigs started to look up he said "okay wait,
don't tell me what you came up with—now I want
you to think of what kind of meat they'd have made
from him?" and the pigs got back to thinking, and
after a little while one of them spoke up and said
"bacon," and another one said "ribs," and another
said "brisket," and then one pig said "TV dinner,"
and some of the pigs laughed and the pig who asked
the question said, "you dumb shit, don't you even
know what a TV dinner is?" and the pig that said it
said "I don't even know what Christ is," and then
all the pigs laughed, and then eventually they all died

just the same, don't you see? the pigs that laughed
and the pig that made them; all just the same,
don't you see? as if they were born to do it
and you're just like oh I don't know maybe
and you're just like oh i see
and then you're just like
I guess that's just
what the plan is.

Milhous

Our friend has this farm out in the western part of the state
where they mostly kill animals and people
often leave animals there they don't want but not the kind
of animals the farm means to kill and so
we end up with one of these unwanted and non-slaughter
animals (a kitten) that our friend saw
sleeping on top of a haystack in the sun just before the summer.
She told us over fried clams about how
there had been a whole litter, and about how the farm's German
shepherd shook out one of the kitten's
brothers or sisters to death, and about how another kitten just
sort of died; just that facts-of-life
kind of stuff. After we got the kitten, the mother ran off somewhere
with the rest of the litter, and
presumably they died in the woods. It took a while to figure it out
but after bottle feeding
the kitten and teaching it how to shit altogether and then how to shit into a box,
and when the kitten
showed proficiency at doing that, we named him Milhous.
Sometimes it's easier, faster
saying that we named him after the cartoon character, but here
I might as well tell the truth that
we named him after Nixon. I figure here was another man obsessed with losing
who through experience learned
how to lose consistently and gracefully. OK yeah, disgracefully, yes, but
it's the kind of thing where you
need to step back and look at it closely. OK, yeah men are terrible; humanity, yes;
men, especially, sure—and here is one
who represents one to one-hundred percent of any of us. OK yeah, my dad

hated Nixon about as much as

he hated cats, but when I told him that we gave Milhous the cat his name (Jack)

as its middle name, he began to ask

about the cat sometimes when he called. I don't believe that my cat is Nixon incarnate,

but I think about it sometimes

when he is testing my patience, when he is doing the things I think he knows

he shouldn't do, but that he feels

so compelled to do, and I curse him. When I see him sleeping, I know that

my mercy keeps him alive,

which reminds me that I've got some mercy in me, and that the world must

have some mercy in it, too,

for there to have been a world with Nixon in it, and now this cat in it.

the Blender

I've been worried about my hair lately
so I've started making smoothies most
mornings, and we got this blender that
is a "quiet" blender because I apparently
can't handle the harshness of this world.

anyway I'm making a peach smoothie
one morning and the blades of the blender
won't catch the ice at the bottom of the
pitcher, and so I try to take the pitcher out
but it unscrews and milk and shit leaks

everywhere. the first thing I do is get
mad at the cat, and then find a towel and
start mopping it up. I shake the pitcher
and try again. still no dice. no smoothie.
at this point I am beside myself furious

with the cat, and jamming a knife down
and in and out of the pitcher trying to
break up anything frozen and basically
performing the function of a blender
albeit not very well, but still somehow

better than the blender itself, so here we
are—and at this point I'm starting to die
a little bit, but I don't really notice it
until after I finally get the blender to work
but before I can have any of the smoothie

I'm dead. now the cat can jump up onto
the counter and drink the smoothie, but
I'm not mad about it (because I am dead
and because everyone who is dead is at
peace I am OK with it all. and St. Peter

is there with a couple of administrators,
and St. Peter welcomes me and I say Hi
and Thanks, and St. Peter says "This isn't
the kind of place where we can just let
any schmuck in off the street," and I nod.

St. Peter says "We need to make sure that
everyone is of the right temperament
before they go anywhere," and I nod.
St. Peter says "Good, so long as you get it.
what's the angriest you've ever been

at a kitchen appliance?" and I feel myself
go cold and St. Peter raises his eyebrows a
bit expectantly a bit mockingly as if to say
HMM? and the administrators start softly
to chuckle a bit and St. Peter hushes them

"Shh! Shut up, shut up," and I look at them
and I shrug and St. Peter says "Well let's
have a look at the tape then, shall we?" and
I shake my head No but he starts it up
regardless though to my relief it isn't the

blender episode, it's something from a
long time ago, my roommate's toaster oven
I was too stoned to figure out. it's all a great
relief until the tape ends and even St. Peter
is laughing now, and he flips a little switch)

and so here I am as a baby set to do this
all over again which some folks would maybe
consider a gift but I'm pretty sad because
the cats and Leah and the smoothie are all
in a life somewhere else in the world and it will

take a while to find the words to find them, but
I might forget about all of that in the process of
finding the words.

'es

        ... of the Delta Sky Miles club
     ... approximately what heaven must be like
i assume

i'm already halfway to heaven, because
of my attitude in saying something like "we are now
members of the Delta Sky Miles club,"

which is to remind you again that that is where
i am, now, and where i belong, i'm sure, for eternity.
but let me tell you a little bit more about what heaven is like.

there are way more people here than
i ever would have thought
and everything is elbows and apologies.

even if the small talk is a kind of hell,
the brevity of formality is a kind of paradise.
there are also a lot of kids up here,

which i guess i should have expected, but
had somehow forgotten, and it's sad;
sad, sad, sad any way you look at it.

you can watch the news up here if you want to
and you can watch your neighbor watch the news.
(the news is no different up here.)

oh also, just so you know, so you can BE PREPARED,
up here in heaven they make you pay for your alcohol
but they don't accept cash

which we had a lifetime to figure out, but
you know, "just another one of those things."
anyway they don't serve Pepsi up here.
is this a surprise? I guess not? but do they serve Pepsi in hell?
rick steves doesn't mention it   the bible doesn't mention it
michelin doesn't mention it   the little video we all watched

showing us all how we're going to die just in case we all die didn't mention it.
is there a place, even in hell, for people who love Pepsi?

maybe not.

oh there I go again—"people." should I be calling us angels? is that what we are now?
up here, down here, wherever it is we go?

maybe not?

the meat here is questionable. you might ask about the vegetarian option,
which is a cheese and fruit plate. that is what I got and it was
pretty good. haha

now that I think of it, the fact that i'm not really a vegetarian
didn't preclude me from getting into heaven
which is sort of disappointing,

spiritually. all that work all that effort all that time
spent thinking about how i could have been
could be doing things differently

all of that apparently
for nothing.

Safe Outside

are you counting going forward are you counting going backward have you kept your eyes closed are they wide do you know yet is it a home or a hiding place it depends on who are you is it branches or is it veins when you open the doors does it rain is it cold do you feel warm enough does she look does he look away do they hold a hand up under your shirt so easy to recognize are you outside have you been how hello where's all the cats where's all the dogs when you open the doors do you see all the people so they say are you inside are you hiding are you home it depends on who you are it depends on where you are it depends on when and who you are when you are there are you predator or prey do your eyes when they open glance around or stay?

                        nd it is licking itself
                             us wet sound of self
care except happier and when it finishes it
sings a little song just like anyone else would
and when it finishes singing its song I ask it:

how does a dog who sings so beautifully
wind up down here in hell? and the dog says
"house pets don't have souls." ohh
come on, I say. and the dog says "I don't make the rules."

so we talk a bit about how we died and I explain
how it was all a big mistake and that it was funny
except that it happened to me and the dog says
"that's rough." and I laugh, is it rough or is it
ruff ruff ruff and the dog says "that's really not
funny actually" and "you know, dogs can't laugh
so jokes are just kind of alienating" and I say
I don't know, it always felt like my dog had a sense
of humor, and the dog says "I'm not your dog, man,
that was your ego" and I say nothing
and you might think that time doesn't pass
yet here we are watching hell move before us
sick as a heart, warm as a heart, solitary in
its usefulness as a heart; silent from the outside.

the dog turns away and throws up and I
do the right thing and pretend not to notice.
the dog says "hey don't worry about that—that's
how I died. I just threw up a bunch
of times and then I was dead" and
"I don't know if it was something they gave me
or if it just kind of happened that way" and I ask
are you ever mad about that?

and the dog says "no"
"I really liked them a lot they held me like they never thought I'd die"
"I wonder if they know what happens"
"I wonder if they know that they're going to die"
"I wonder if it's not going to be for a while that they die"
"I hope it's not for a while"
"I hope they don't throw up a lot when they die"
and "I hope that if they do that it at least tastes great"

and the last part seems to give the dog some peace
but not me, I'm still pretty sad although maybe
just a little dehydrated. then I say to the dog
it sounds like you like throwing up, do you like
throwing up? and the dog says "I like lots of things"
and then it says "want to go and see if we can find
your dog?" and I say No because I don't know how
to say how I am scared we might find her and I never
really thought about what we do with our dogs after
we've put them away.

Big Bird Singing at His Father's Funeral

I don't know how to be like Big Bird singing
when he sang at Jim Henson's funeral.
How to hide the obvious human inside of something
obviously very much more obvious.

How do I suspend your disbelief that I am there;
I am here? How would my ability to misunderstand
help you to understand? How could my childishness
be put to some use?

I don't know if I know how to teach or to entertain.
I don't know if my green but growing handle on letters,
colors, numbers, and time could be put to use maybe—
I really don't. Please

don't lose your patience with me. Try to let me act it out.
Let me close my eyes and make up a prayer,
even if I'm only just feeling sorry for myself a little bit,
or even if it's only crib talk: the kind of talk we talk

with god; secret, alone and in the dark,
grownups pass outside the room speaking
softly as they do trying not to wake us
as they go—I don't know.

Whatever is sad let it be sad.
Whatever you think you have, think that.
Sometimes it's hard to feel like you have something.
Sometimes everything feels sad.

Sometimes it feels like you're a great big yellow thing
and you have to do something you need to do but
not want to be seen, and you wonder, maybe you hope
they don't see you here singing, yet you wonder if
he can't hear you down here singing there like that.

Happy New Year from the Reptile Lagoon Dillon, SC

It's a brand new year and
just before morning
and I'm here looking down at
the Reptile Lagoon

an empty parking lot lit red by
a sign that says
"Reptile Lagoon" outside a small
building and I imagine

it probably stinks in there really
bad, like hell, kind of
like the flamingo enclosure
at the Stone Zoo,

back when they still had a
flamingo enclosure.
I hardly remember going there—
if not for this moment

I may have entirely forgotten.
Maybe the whole zoo
smelled that way. Or maybe everything
smells like that and

I didn't notice until I visited the zoo.
You say Happy New Year
and take a picture
and it's one of me smiling, standing

in front of this sign,
building and parking lot. If this was
all there was, the end
of the world, you could know.

You take a few more
in case one of them is bad;
in case my smile had changed;
in case you ever looked at them again

and you had to pick one.

Acknowledgements

This publication is made possible through the generosity and support of the DeSimone English Endowment created by Midge DeSimone '76 and Thomas DeSimone. A deep thanks to Brooke Delp and M.P. Carver for their work on layout and design.

These poems or earlier versions first appeared in the following journals:

PATRICIA CALLAN
"Mirrors" *Unstamatic*
"On My Eighteenth Birthday, My Friend Gave Me a Playgirl Magazine" *Adanna*

M.P. CARVER
"C A P I T A L I S M" *Fox Chase Review*

JD DEBRIS
"The Voice of Hercules" *Ninth Letter*
"Those 'Mexicans For Golovkin' Shirts" *Cincinnati Review*
"Le Bonheur" *Freezeray*
"Bossa Nova Was Invented In a Bathroom" *Freezeray*
"One For Adán" *Salamander*
"Beverly Grove" *The Adroit Journal*
"Drunk With the Mermaid" *Invisible City*
"On Future Rhyming…" *Narrative*
"New York, 2020" *Minnesota Review*

CATHERINE FAHEY
"Inishmore" *Dime Show Review*
"Crewel" *Postcard Poems and Prose*
"The External Soul" *The Bitchin' Kitsch*
"Gold as Straw" *Ghost City Review*

"The Roses that Bloom at the End of the World" *The Raven Chronicles*
"Queen of Swords" *Coffin Bell*
"Page of Cups" *Coffin Bell*
"Eight of Cups" *Haunted: Tarot Poems eChapbook*
"Ornithomancy" *Boston Accent Lit*

GREGORY GLENN
"dog" *Soundings East*
"wild." *Poetry Soup Magazine*
"Safe Outside" *Poetry Soup Magazine*
"The Blender" *Drunk Monkeys*
"Big Bird Singing at His Father's Funeral" *Drunk Monkeys*

About the Poets

Patricia Callan lives in Beverly, MA with husband, daughters, and a teeny-tiny beagle. In addition to writing, she also loves to teach and make mixed-media art. Her work can be found at *Hawaii Pacific Review*, *Unstamatic*, *Adanna Literary Journal*, *Drunk Monkeys*, *Dream Pop Press*, and *Mom Egg Review*.

M.P. Carver is a poet and visual artist from Salem, MA. She is an editor at YesNo Press, miCrO-Founder of the journal *Molecule: a tiny lit mag*, former poetry editor of *Soundings East*, and Director of the 2021 Massachusetts Poetry Festival. Her work has appeared in *The Lily Poetry Review*, *Jubilat*, and *50Haikus*, among others. Her chapbook, *Selachimorpha*, was published by Incessant Pipe in 2015.

JD Debris writes poems, songs, and prose. He held the Goldwater Fellowship at NYU from 2018–20, where he completed his MFA. In 2020 his work was chosen by Ilya Kaminsky for *Ploughshares*'s Emerging Writers Prize, and he was named to *Narrative*'s 30 Below 30 list. His releases include the chapbook *Sparring* (Salem State University Press, 2018) and the music albums *Black Market Organs* (Simple Truth Records, 2017) and *JD Debris Murder Club* (forthcoming).

Catherine Fahey is a poet and librarian from Salem, Massachusetts. When she's not reading and writing, she's knitting or dancing. Her debut chapbook, *The Roses that Bloom at the End of the World*, is available from Boston Accent Lit. You can read more of her work at magpiepoems.com.

Gregory Glenn is a writer and artist from Massachusetts. He is Beloved Editor Supreme at *Unpopular Writer*, and former poetry editor for *Soundings East*. His work has been featured in *Poetry Soup*, *Drunk Monkeys*, and through Mass Poetry. In 2019, his collection, *Poems*, was awarded a Joseph T. Flibbert prize. He frequently collaborates with actor Jeff Marcus, performing together as Greg&Jeff.